This book is dedicated to Frankles & Nomi without whom this would be proper Mills & Boon Shite

Jeanette's story

Nobody wanted to work in the Albion street library on a Wednesday. To be honest very few people wanted to work in the Library at all and of those that did you had to be desperate or stupid to agree to work a Wednesday afternoon. Jeanette was certainly not stupid, so that must make her desperate, desperate for the finer things in life, the clothes, the cars and the status that came with wealth. Not that anyone ever got wealthy working as a part time librarian but it covered her rent and the cost of hair extensions, by working the Wednesday she even brought home enough to cover the expensive gym membership she needed to keep her toned nineteen year old body in shape.

The library alone however was never going to keep Jeanette in the manner that she wished, and having not been born with a silver spoon in her mouth, living with her Dad who was a delivered potatoes for a living Jeanette was under no illusions that if she wanted the finer things in life she was going to have to work for it. It was her friend Cheryl in the early hours of her nineteenth birthday who had first suggested Jeanette take up babysitting, not immediately impressed with the return for looking after snivelling kids Cheryl had gone onto explain that with Jeanette's killer arse, long legs and pretty face there were plenty of ways of getting a little extra from the Dad's during a lift home.

Jeanette had a new client, and from what she could gather from the internet he was worth a bob or two, Jeanette anticipated relieving him of a couple of hundred quid beyond the £30 she charged for the babysitting, Some called it Prostitution, others escorting to Jeanette it was just business and looking at the slightly smarmy looking accountant who's children she was looking after that evening he looked just the sort to be in need of some relief.

The alarm of Jeanette's watch began to urgently bleep, 5 minutes to go she thought reaching under the library counter for the air fresher, she swished her long platinum blonde hair back from her neck and sashayed through the library spraying a liberal dose before ducking into the staff locker room where she quickly changed from her thigh skimming skirt to a pair of jeans and a polo neck. Retrieving a tube of Vicks nasal rub from her fake Prada handbag she rubbed a small amount of the strong smelling ointment under her nose as she returned to the counter. Here we go she thought as the plastic clock clicked onto two o'clock and the chine of the entry bell hanging above the front door sounded.

Roger's story

Roger was in a rush and pissed off, having had to spend the day in Leeds shopping with his wife, Ann and two kids Mark and Sally, who had both been desperate to assist his wife in melting his various credit cards, he was desperate to get home. Roger had plans for tonight and he wanted to have a shower, leave the kids in the care of the babysitter he had been told about by one of the blokes from the office and get out for a meal with Ann, followed all being well with a chance to fuck the babysitter on the way home. Roger was an accountant, the head of his own department and liked to think he was going places, despite a sizeable mortgage his knowledge of tax law and as he liked to think of it 'an eye for a chance' meant he could afford to let his family blow the credit cards every once in a while, and still have access to funds to enjoy the finer things in life. That's why his Range rover had 'over finch' in red on the rear boot lid, why he had a Rolex Yacht master on his left wrist, and why blowing a couple of hundred quid to get his nob wet was not a problem. However the way he saw it getting his nob wet was more of an investment than a luxury. Glancing over at his wife who at ten years his junior was perhaps possessed one of his better investments, a great pair of plastic tits.

Eric's story

"Gerr art t'way theur cunt" Spat Eric as he was forced to apply the brakes to his Daf Lf45 lorry, as a curtain sider pulled into his lane, it was difficult to signal while rolling a fag, and keeping time to Oh you pretty things. Eric pulled into lane two, causing the topless Hawaiian dancer to wobble from side to side, and the Range rover alongside him to break sharply throwing Mum, Dad and the two kids forward in their harnesses. Eric's elderly diesel engine let out a spew of fumes for them to chew on as he effectively blocked the Eastbound A63. Eric nodded along to his favourite Bowie track and thought back to his days as a roadie for the spiders from Mars. Tucking the long straggly hair that had escaped his bandana behind an ear and holding it in place with his finished roll up, Eric was impervious to the horns of derision from the score of motorists he was now delaying. Eric Joined in with the chorus "you gotta make way for the homo superior" They were behind him, He was on his way to Hull's Hessle road, and he didn't give a shite.

Foxy's story

Foxy Loveless entered the library and grinned, He loved Wednesday. Wednesday was his library day and the blonde woman was here. Smiling at her his piggy eyes greedily ran up her body taking in her long legs, pert tits and full lips, Foxy knew she had a nice arse tucked in below the counter and as was his Wednesday tradition wondered what colour underwear she was wearing. None he thought immediately picturing the librarian as he always did blouse undone, skirt rucked up above her keens with her legs spread over the counter, allowing him to examine her. His grin widened. Shuffling his feet encased against the spores in plastic bags towards the counter he rummaged in the deep pockets of his once green jacket pulling out a selection of used crispy tissues a few tom cards depicting scantily clad beauties and their contact phone numbers and depositing them on the counter, "twoa 'rs ont' internet" he spluttered blowing out saliva, fetid breath and lunch onto the counter he slapped the fiver down on the counter which as always the librarian picked up by an edge as though it was contaminated with her perfectly manicured hand. What she didn't know grinned Foxy was that this time it was contaminated, he'd spunked on it.

Rogers Story

Distracted momentarily by his wife's cleavage Roger looked up as his wife suddenly stiffened up in her seat, noticing as he did her dress rising up her slim thighs high enough to see the tops of the stockings he insisted she wear, "Shite" he mumbled stepping hard on the Range rovers breaks as a Lorry swung out in front of him Blaring his horn the dashboard of his vehicle flashed its ABS warning light to him as the low sun caught the rear of the waggon in front of him, "did you see that fucking moron" He said incredulously bringing the vehicle under control and vigorously flashing his lights down the outside of the lorry which was now slowing him down. "Not in front of the kids dear" she replied, Glancing in the rear view mirror Roger could see the sullen faces of his two kids, each with headphones plugged into their IPad's, and despite thinking to himself that there was fat chance they will have heard him decided not to continue the conversation with Ann, knowing that with her fiery disposition any conversation could lead to an argument and with it being Wednesday he didn't want to piss his wife off any more than was necessary. Wednesday was his night for a bit of over the side shagging and if his wife was in a bad mood all his plans could be scuppered.

As traffic built up behind him Roger glanced up reading for the first time the legend emblazoned upon the rear doors, "Let Eric drop his load in your kitchen" It proudly proclaimed; Eric is a cunt thought Roger as finally the lorry cleared the front of the articulated vehicle it was passing and would now be able to pull in, "come on then" He muttered again flashing his lights angrily at the rear of the lorry which only now slowly began to swing to the left, stepping on the gas the surge of the turbo carried his vehicle alongside the lorry where he could see the driver who looked like some sort of rocker hippy arsehole to Roger giving him the wanker sign from the cab, leaning across his wife Roger stuck his middle finger up at the lorry driver at the same time noticing that his arm was leaning across Ann's chest, drawing his hand slowly back and straitening up Roger trailed his fingers slowly over the twin mounds of his wife's chest; She didn't say anything and as he straightened up in his seat, Roger took as second to make room in his trousers for the semi, the tits he had bought his wife had created. In the door pocket his mobile chimed.

?

Eric's story

Ten minutes later delayed by the lack of power in his engine, and the weight of several hundred sacks of spuds in his load, Eric finally had room to pull back in, delaying as long as he could just to further fuck off the twat in the driving seat of the Range rover who had been all over the back of him since he had pulled out he returned to lane one, watching the sudden acceleration from the black range rover as it moved to overtake him he muttered "Theur can peyt to soon son, li thy Dad" and began to wave his right arm in the international signal of the wanker through his side window, As the vehicle came alongside him he glanced down into the passenger seat to see flash of shapely stocking clad thigh and a cracking bit of cleavage, . All Eric noticed of the driver was the sun glinting off the frames of his glasses and that the bald spot on the back of his head was now blocking his view of the tits. The driver, leaning across his passenger was also displaying a hand signal indicating his appreciation of Eric's driver. Probably hasn't given her a good seen to in years thought Eric as disregarding the no smoking signs the law required him to have in his cab he lit his roll up and puffed happily away as the range rover lead the other 15 cars his manoeuvre had delayed past him. Glancing at his knock off Rolex he saw it was just two o'clock, even with the traffic building for rush hour he should be done by seven he figured just in time to grab a bite to eat before seeing what was on offer for the night in Hessle road.

Foxy's story

www.freepornslags.com/dirtybitches

Foxy undid the string holding the zipless crotch of his grime incrusted trousers together clicked on the website and began to wank

Jeanette's story

Thank god thought Jeanette as the stinking vagrant shuffled over towards where the computers were sat, Although she didn't mind working Wednesdays for the free time it gave her to organise her other employments She hated the smell of the man who had entered Something Loveless was his name and to Jeanette he certainly looked it, What the fuck are those plastic bags about she wondered as her thumb skimmed the keypad of her phone, "Would you be ok to give me a lift home tonight? I'm only young and I would hate someone to take advantage of me" Almost as soon as she had put her phone down it chimed "Don't worry I'll bring protection ;)" Hmmm naughty thought Jeanette spotting the double meaning, her fingers slipping over the keys in rapid time "Oooh I like a big manly man with £200 in his back pocket" she accompanied the text with a photo from her collection of risqué selfies on her phone of the one straight down her cleavage, knowing that this one was a done deal. In order to save face with this blokes unsuspecting wife she would have to sit through a couple of hours with kids who hopefully would be asleep so she could make better use of her time, a couple of minutes bouncing up and down on some middle age blokes lap and she would be quid's in. Trying to ignore the noises coming from the public access computer area she brought up her internet banking. Kerching she thought looking at the balance.

Brenda's story

The Plaice was doing a roaring trade as usual for a Wednesday evening and all 220lb of Brenda was sweating, "Jont salt 'n vinegar on 'em" she said automatically while simultaneously loading a large haddock and a mound of chips onto the paper in front of her. Wiping a man size hand across her forehead giving the customer ample opportunity to inspect her damp pits resplendent with a grey fuzz of stubble she set her cheap hoop earrings a dangling. "'a will be three quid eighty" she said automatically. Reaching round to liberate a small acre of trouser material from where it was wedged between her massive arse cheeks, Her latest customer sidled out of the chippie allowing a welcome breath of fresh air to waft in from outside before it to became polluted by the ripe mixture of hot chips, fish Brenda's cheap perfume and arse crack. Wafting the front of her tunic unsticking it from her dugs Brenda felt itchy, she hoped it was just a reaction to grease and sweat and not another round of crabs. Reaching down with her left hand she lifted her paunch before sliding her right hand into the top of her cheap elasticated trousers, giving herself a hard vigorous rub through her knickers she enjoyed the springy feeling of the pubes pushing against the damp fabric of her underwear. Brenda hadn't had a good seeing to for a fortnight, since Eric the Potato man had last dropped his load and she was frustrated. Fuck it she thought; a little warm up and she reached for a battered sausage dipped it in the gravy and waddled through to the back room.

Foxy's story

Foxy let out a low moan as he came hot cum splashing against the bottom of the desk above his rancid cock, after a few moments to get his breath back Foxy stood zipped up and slithered out of the library. Scanning around he noticed it was starting to get dark, Ignoring all those around him who did their best to get out of his way Foxy let rip, phlegm barely missing a passing shoe. He wandered off towards the alleyway at the back of the Italian where he knew it was warm.

Ann's Story

Ann was bored with the crappy Italian she found herself sat in for what felt like the nine millionth time. Ever since they had met Roger had been bringing her to this hole with its checked red white and green table cloths, signed football pictures and baskets of supermarket own brand breadsticks, She didn't understand why they needed to come here every Wednesday before she let Roger off the leash for a night, but it seemed to work for Roger and with the money his extracurricular activities was bringing in she wasn't going to complain. As Roger waffled on about some shite or other her mind wandered to her main passion in life Camera work, she began as she always did looking around the room, trying to ascertain where she would place the cameras and lighting if she had to shoot a scene in the restaurant. Strange she thought to herself as she mentally added up what equipment she would need to complete her set; why is it I always want to film a porno in here

Rogers Story

As she stood up Roger as he always did sneaked a quick look down the top of her low dress before watching her walk away across the crowded restaurant the swing of her hips and the tightness of her arse as always setting off the thought that at least Ann put the expensive gym membership to good use, whilst at the same time triggering a semi. Reaching for his phone he fired off a quick one line text message

"I've got a massive boner. Shame to waste it?"

Ann's story

Hearing the distinctive chirp of her mobile phone Ann was distracted reaching into her handbag as she approached the swing door leading to the back corridor where the ladies was situated, as she put her hand out to push the door it suddenly moved away from her, stumbling forward she took an involuntary step through the door before coming up hard against a body. A man's body she felt a powerful arm wrap around her pulling her tight against what felt like a wall of muscle.

Erics Story

Sated with a kebab, and can of Stella and in no rush to return to his crummy bedsit Eric was crawling his lorry slowly down Hessle Road It was still early for the girls but Eric knew that desperation would have driven one or two of them out into the cold winters evening. Eric liked to pride himself on being a man for any lady, rather than a ladies man, Size, age, looks were unimportant to him pulse optional he told himself and anyone who would listen at regular intervals. On his nearside he saw a woman stood on the junction to a side road, Eric grinned as he gave her the once over as he approached, Wrong side of 40, tight mini skirt, fishnets, knee high fuck me boots and that resigned air only a working girl could muster. "It's thy lucky neet" He grinned slowing down next to the woman who was already lowering the zipper on her moth eaten probably fake fur coat. Winding down his window Eric's date shouted up "Eur theur lookin for business love" to Eric's ears her forty Bensons a day gravelly voice was like music "aye darlin op on I' a' much for eur nosh off"

As she climbed in and grinned at him Eric looked past the cold sore on the corner of her mouth "Fifteen for eur blowy, thirty for full fex ah'm not doin amal t'need as uz arse is rotten bur normally that's eur tenna extreur" rasped the Tom "sounds jannock" grinned back Eric noticing for the first time she had false teeth "Doa thy teeth cum art if sa ah'm well up for just eur blowie" The tom grinned and pulled out the top row of her teeth, smiling at Eric she said "babby ah can suk li' eur fookin oova bur it's twenty wiyaa uz teeth" Eric grinned showing the tom his rows of yellowing canines, and spluttered "Fookin' 'ell that's steep does thee think ah'm made o' brass" The tom ran her ulcerated tongue across the thin gummy "Ah fuk it gerr ya laughin clobba aroun' dis" Eric said unbuttoned his fly and pulled his cock free of his trousers "Ah dooant doa

discahts for tiddlers theur norrz" grinned the Tom holding out her
hand for the money.

Ann's Story

Ann's first reaction was to pull away but then she looked up recognising the new member of the waiting staff, the one with the deep dark eyes and the ready smile that she had noticed when Roger had been pointing out to him which was their usual tables. She couldn't remember his name but as that same smile spread across his face she suddenly found she couldn't remember much else either. "I am sorry Madam" his voice purred in her ear instantly raising a flush across her chest and quickening her heartrate, instinctively her hips pressed forward against him. Taking a step back, allowing the door to swing close and screen them from the diners, the waiter tightened his grip around Ann's waist crushing her breasts against his chest. Ann felt him begin to stir and she rotated her hips slowly grinding them against the waiter feeling his cock against her stomach.

Suddenly a door opened at the other end of the corridor and they broke apart guiltily Ann was breathless "I shall try to be more careful inze future madam" He said, "This door can be very dangerous" Ann muttered something about it being her fault before quickly escaping to the sanctuary of the ladies room. She was shaking she realised as she looked at herself in the mirror, splashing water on her face she realised that both her nipples were stuck out like marbles and she could feel the slick moisture between her thighs, Locking herself into a cubicle Ann began to frantically search through the contents of her handbag looking for the magic bullet vibrator she normally carried everywhere with her, her frustration mounting as she realised that she had forgotten to take it out of her spongebag following a recent business trip. Deciding to switch to manual she leant back against the wall pulling her skirt up to her waist and slid her black lace underwear to one side. With one hand tugging on her left nipple and she slid her middle finger into her tight wet hole before using her thumb and forefinger to search out the firm button of her clit, Ann imagined that the waiter was in the cubicle with her, Imagined his head between her legs his tongue on her slit. The pressure of her orgasm began to build she tilted her head back biting her bottom lip to stop a moan escaping her lips; Crash the ladies room door went back on its Hinges heavy footsteps sounded across the tiles followed by a shudder as a large weight settled itself into the cubicle next door, Ann jolted out of her fantasy guiltily removed jerked her fingers from her soaking slit, Sulphur assaulted her nostrils and the grunts and splashes of what sounded like a fully grown mountain gorilla having its first shite in a week assailed her senses. Gagging she rearranged her clothing she escaped the cubicle, as she was checking herself in the mirror the Gorilla Spoke "Soz Love, ah nearly Shi missen theear" The voice boomed foghorn like from inside the other cubicle, Not wanting to spend any longer in the ladies which was rapidly becoming a health hazard Ann beat a quick retreat back to her table.

🤷

Eric's story

Peeling off two tenner's and handing them to her Eric leaned back in his chair and lit his roll up as the tom scuttled over and lowered her head over his cock which was already hard. Grasping it firmly by the root she pulled back the Eric's foreskin unleashing the unmistakeable smell of unwashed cock. Even with the damage done my years of narcotic misuse the Tom tried not to gag as her gummy lips slithered over the end of Eric's nob "Suk it then theur sag" Eric murmured romantically " ah'm not payin theur ta kiss t' fookin' thin" The tom increased her suction running her gummy lips down the length of Eric's knob burying her head into his pubes, Reaching down Eric lifted his belly slightly allowing the Tom to swallow the last inch of his dick resting his belly on her head Eric sighed his contentment taking a deep suck on his rollup as the Tom tried not to breath. She began to shuttle up and down Eric's cock increasing the suction, unbeknown to her in her desperation to get done this was turning into the best blowjob Eric had ever had and within moments he was getting a sweat on "Sweet Jesus theur dirty bitch ah goan cum enny fookin' secon" As the Tom Began to pull away Eric clamped one of his huge palms across the back of her head pulling her down onto his cock "Let uz nip on or ill bi' t' fookin' thin off" she slobbered around a mouth full of cock "Aye bi' daahn theur gormless ca theur getten neya teeth I" realising she was trapped the Tom gave one last powerful suck the length of Eric's cock and with a shudder he came, the wave of cum hit the back of the Toms throat and for once she didn't try to suppress the gag reflex letting go of a stomach full of half-digested cum all over Eric's cock and lap. "Ah theur dirty fookin' bitch why did theur doa 'a" Pushing her across the cab the Tom laughed "That's t' smallest cock I' seen orl week theur fookin' clart noggin" With that she slipped from the cab and ran off down a ginnel. Reaching over for one of the paper serviettes he got with his Kebab Eric began to wipe himself off,

Brenda will give that a good cleaning tomorrow he thought to himself before suddenly screaming out in pain as the smear of chilli sauce connected to his bell end.

Brenda's Story

Brenda struggled out of her trousers and perched on the edge of a freezer, "Bloody ell teur parky" she muttered as her ample arse spread across the cold metal lid, dragging her greying bloomers to her knees, spreading her legs she absentmindedly licked the dribble of gravy running off the battered sausage and across the back of her hand. The lips of her labia bulged outwards spreading them with her left hand she aimed the makeshift dildo at her gaping slit and pushed it home letting out a satisfied little fart Brenda worked the sausage deep into her using the knuckles of her hand against her clit. "Ah a feels gran" she wheezed breathlessly closing her eyes and thinking of Eric, As her pleasure mounted she began to make little grunting noises rolling the sausage in ever increasing circles knuckles deep inside her, within a minute her eyes rolled back and a line of drool slid from the corner of her mouth, she felt her cunt muscles contract around the meaty snack. The knobbles of the dried batter rubbing against her clit proved too much and throwing her head back, braying; horse like she came with a hacking cough. Grobing a phlegm into the corner she slid off the freezer wiping the mixture of Grease, gravy and her own juices off the freezer lid she dragged her trousers back into place and sidled back into the shop, slipping the sausage back into the warming cupboard she glanced at the clock, Well that killed a bit of time she thought sniffing her fingers as the chime of the doorbell rang out. Stepping to the counter Brenda glared at the young girl who had walked in, half her age, quarter of her weight and with tits that didn't point to the floor Brenda took an instant dislike to the young girl and scowled "Wha' can ah gerr theur" she growled. "Oh just a battered sausage" replied the youth. Brenda smiled.

▣ Jeanette's story

Babysitting was fucking boring thought Jeanette, The kids had gone straight to bed and despite the battered sausage she had gobbled down on the way over she was hungry, the parents of the kids had not said anything to her about not making herself a snack hunting out the kitchen Jeanette stumbled across the utility room hunger forgotten her eyes were drawn to the washing machine throbbing away in a corner. Knowing she faced an evening of disappointment she grinned "well a girl has to take her pleasure where she can" she said out loud, pulling the door closed behind her, she undid the button on the side of her plaited skirt letting it fall to the floor exposing her black suspender belt, stockings and G string combo, kicking off her shoes she leant forward resting her plump mound against the corner of the throbbing machine feeling the cold metal through the thin material of her G string; leaning forward over the back of the machine she lifted her right leg rubbing her clit against the rounded corner of the machine. The rocking of the machine began to send warm pulses directly to her clit and she gasped out loud, with her left hand she pulled out a pert tit from her short vest and squeezed the nipple erect using pressure that fluctuated on the border between pleasure and pain, her breathing stared to become more and more ragged as the machine droned on

With a short beep the programme on the washing machine kicked on a notch, and the spin cycle started the machine spinning its load faster and faster as the damp load began to shed water Jeanette was getting wetter and vibrations of the machine were becoming more and more intense, reaching a hand down between her body and the cold metal of the machine she lifted her ass up into the air and pulled the damp material of her G string to one side giving her access to her lubricated snatch, her left hand tugging desperately on her nipple she flicked her bean slowly contrasting the deep vibrations of the machine beneath her to the sharp pressure of her hands, scratching her manicured nails along the landing strip of her Brazilian she rode the machine harder and harder as her breath became ragged, tilting her head back to the ceiling and letting out a primeval moan she came hard drenching her hand and the top of the machine with her come. Her eyes were unseeing and she was lost totally in the moment as her clit quivered and the muscles in her cunt clenched. No sooner had her orgasm passed than another one rushed up on her as the machine threatened to throw her to the floor "Fuuuucccckkkk" she cried as the second if anything more intense orgasm jolted through her, on weakening legs Jeanette sank to the floor and sat back against a cupboard door, breathing heavily and just a little sweaty Jeanette watched as a dribble of moisture slithered down the side of the washing machine, leaning forward her tiny pink tongue darted out and lapped her cunt juices from the machine.

Ann's Story

Roger smiled that supercilious little smile of his as she sat down opposite him, she saw that he had been using his phone while she had been gone, no doubt playing one of those stupid little games he was always waffling about she thought. "do you want some pud" asked Roger lifting his arm into the air and clicking his fingers "Oi garcon" He yelled Ann Horrified noticed the waiter walking towards them from across the room, His eyes locked onto her, She felt herself begin to flush, as she remembered her fantasy, Don't be a little girl she chided herself meeting his eyes directly with her own and smiling over Rogers shoulder invitingly at him "Its cameriere dear" she said tartly "What is?" replied Roger "Waiter is dear, in Italian, Garcon is French" The waiter reached the table looming over them smiled replying "That is correct madam, you even have the accent right" "Who cares" Roger droned annoyed at having been shown up by his wife "we would like to see the desert list" He snapped The waiter smiled and backed away returning moments later this time standing closer to Ann's side of the table, he handed Roger the leather covered menu before looking down at Ann and "And here is a package for madam" "It's a fucking menu" Roger quipped but Ann didn't hear him, as she sat her eyes were on a level with and mere inches from the significant bulge in the waiters trousers, "It's a big package" She said reluctantly lifting her vision staring back at the waiter she parted her lips slightly knowing he could see straight down her dress, Taking the menu her gaze returned to the now growing bulge in his trousers Ann figured she could hear the strain on his zipper even over Roger whining "Menu it's not a package it's a menu. " I shall give you a moment to decide said the waiter backing away" "Arsehole" muttered Roger picking up his phone, "Darling I'll have the tiramisu but I'm just popping outside for a cigarette" Said Ann picking up her handbag, Roger ignored her so she glided through the restaurant and out onto the cold street. It was blustery out on the main road, so Ann hurried around the corner and down a side alleyway, It was dark lit only by the tiny green light of the restaurants fire escape sign above the raised side door to the Italian, It was cold and the air was scented with the smell of frying garlic and stale rubbish, fumbling with her lighter and cigarette Ann jumped as a voice close by said "allow me" he waiter sauntered over He towered over Ann even in her heels reaching out to her he clicked his lighter moving closer to her so she could light her cigarette "I hope you are enjoying your evening madam" He said standing close to her, " I would be doing if I wasn't here with my Husband" Ann replied The waiter shifter and stood closer to her "Madam if you don't mind me asking, but you are a very beautiful woman, why are you here with that Man, you could do so much better for yourself" " Ann reached forward dropping her cigarette as she did so and ran her fingers slowly down the waiters chest "Hmm maybe I could find a younger man" she whispered as her fingers traced down his shirt and lightly traced the outline of his cock. The waiter spun her round stretched out her arms and pinned her against the cold hard wall of the restaurant, It was dark but Ann could make out the reflection of the emergency light in his eyes She lifted up a knee and flicked it from side to side across his crotch, The waiter switched his grip pinning her effortlessly against the wall with one hand and with the other now free began to undo the three buttons restraining her breasts. Their mouth collided, engulfed each other, he cupped his hand under her right breast and lifted if free from her dress, She wasn't wearing a bra, he moved back slightly so that he could lower his mouth to her large brown nipple and sucked it into his mouth, The change in temperature between the cold air and his hot mouth made Ann gasp and her breath became heavier as she started to squeeze his cock through the thin material of his trousers, pulling her arm free from his grip she tugged on his belt loosening it before slipping open the button and lowering the fly, Now it was the waiters turn to gasp, as Ann's hand burrowed into his pants and cupped his balls, Ann began to tug at his rapidly expanding cock, It felt huge to Ann when compared to Rogers tiny knob. She felt the waiter slide his hands up her thigh over her stocking tops and hitch her skirt up around her waist, His hot mouth left her breath she felt him kiss down her body sinking to his knees in front of her, She shifted her legs apart to make it easier for him, feeling his hot breath on her pussy, he slid her already damp underwear to one side and slowly licked her moist slip before sliding one then another finger into her before pulling them back towards him. Ann wrapped her fingers into his thick black hair lost in the moment she recognised that her fantasy could never have been as good as this, Suddenly her eyes flew wide. Goose bumps popped up all over her exposed body, she felt eyes on her.

Foxy's story

Having settled down for the night deep in the alleyway Foxy had begun to slumber, however the experience of 15 years living rough meant that Foxy was never truly asleep and suddenly the low voices of a man and a woman startled him awake, silently he burrowed out of the pile of rubbish he was using as insulation and took in the sight in front of him. Foxy's eyes shot wide; tonight it would appear he had front row seats. Foxy saw the man pressing the woman up against the side of the alleyway, saw her lifting her dress and his hand sliding up her thigh, as he bent to take a nipple into his mouth he began to salivate as he watched the man taste her pussy juices. Without taking his eyes off the action Foxy began to undo the string on his trousers, his cock growing harder by the second.

Ann's Story

"Is something the matter" murmured the waiter his head still buried under her skirt, Ann's eyes darted everywhere was someone watching her, she had felt sure of it a moment ago, perhaps it was paranoia, the fear of her husband being so close by, "No, No everything's fine She gasped" the feeling of being watched although receding now had excited her and she felt electric, using his hair she pulled the waiter to his feet and kissed him tasting her own juices on his lips as she thrust her tongue sinuously into his mouth, pulling his now rock hard cock out from his pants. Ann climbed him wrapping her long silken legs around his hips and seeking for his cock, pulling her arms above her head one time, the waiter bucked his hips and guided by Ann he head of his cock slip teasingly against Ann's slit, she moaned as it brushed against her clit, trying once again to guide it into her "I want you inside me" She whispered, The waiter grunted and thrust his hips hard pushing through her resistance into the wet heat, Ann's eyes flew open, as he thrust into her to the hilt filling her completely, She tightened her legs around him as his mouth again found her nipple, he slid almost totally out of her and Ann before again forcing himself deep into her, Ann Moaned her eyes closed her mouth slack as she ground herself against his cock, working herself up to an orgasm, The waiter played with her taking her to the brink, letting her grind against him one moment before suddenly withdrawing leaving her empty and throbbing right on the brink "I need to come" she breathed frustrated now by his game "Soon" he panted his hot breath steaming in the cold air, Ann tightened her legs once more around him and he began to fuck her harder and harder her orgasm mounted and she came hard just as the fire door above her crashed open, "Yeah fuck knows where she's got to" blasted Roger's dulcet tones "She's probably having a crap again or something" Anna's eyes flew wide as feet below where her husband leant on the banister rail she was impaled on another man's cock. "What tonight, erm yes I mean sure that's fine, you're going to do what exactly" Roger continued his phone conversation as the waiter again began to move inside Anna slowly and then faster pounding into her, with muted wet slaps, Ann couldn't move and despite the fear of getting caught found her body responding again, she sucked the waiters tongue into her mouth and squeezed her love muscles around his cock, tighter she knew he breathed into her mouth and deep inside her Ann felt his cock twitch and jerk as warm cum filled her and set of her own orgasm stifling her scream in his shoulder.

Jeanette's story

Jeanette picked herself up off the floor and rummaged through the cupboards, finding a bottle of Bacardi breezer in the back of the fridge she popped the cap off and wandered back through to the lounge, looking at her watch she wondered where Roger & Ann had got to she was now desperate to get on with the real reason she was here this evening and then get home to do some washing of her own. She decided after their text flirting earlier that Roger was a sure thing, and that it was time to lay her cards on the table, folding herself into an armchair she dialled his number. Roger answered on the second ring telling Jeanette to wait as he was still in the restaurant, Jeanette could hear the hustle and bustle of the busy restaurant followed by the slam of a metal door being pushed open. "are you with me now baby" she said, "Yes" replied Roger "fuck knows where she has got to She's probably having a crap again or something" Jeanette smiled, it was so easy she thought as she stretched her tight young body feeling the residual heat in her core "She replied It's not just babysitting you know baby, I can cock sit as well if you like" She smiled to herself as Roger began to splutter and stammer down the phone "What tonight, erm yes I mean sure that's fine, you're going to do what exactly" Jeanette then began to describe in minute detail exactly what she was going to do with Roger who from the tone of his voice suggested he was going to cum any second sat in the restaurant or otherwise, she signed off the call moments later, pointing out that she was a busy girl and that time was money. The stage set she took a swig of her drink straightened her suspender belt and sat back to enjoy the wide screen TV.

Ann's story

The waiters cock eventually started to wilt and Anna uncrossed her legs from behind his back and returning to the ground let his cock slip out of her, she felt his cum dribble down her leg, She heard the fire door bang shut as her husband returned to the restaurant Sliding her underwear off her leg she used it to clean herself before throwing them into the darkness of the alleyway, the waiter was rearranging his own clothing so she gave him one last lingering kiss before heading back in through the front door of the restaurant. Joining her husband at the table, she suggested they skip pudding and go home Roger assuming his wife was in the mood eagerly settled up the bill and escorted her back to their range rover parked nearby, as they drove away from the restaurant Ann looked out of the window, and saw a dark figure scurrying rat like down the road.

Foxy's story

Foxy could not believe his luck, front row seats to his own private porno, and now having checked the cost was clear he lumbered out of his hiding place and dashed across the uneven litter strewn alleyway before singing to his knees and reverently picking up the discarded piece of silk. Holding it up to his face Foxy luxuriated in the feel of the smooth damp fabric between his fingers and took a deep breath, even over the combination of the rancid alley and his own fetid smell Foxy could smell the sex on the knickers, Quickly worried his treasure would be taken from him he scampered from the alleyway rushing through the damp night towards the deserted house he sometimes slept in. Checking in his pocket for his treasure and surreptitiously stroking his cock through his trousers he scurried down the darkened streets

Rogers & Jeanette's story

Roger was heavy on the breaks as he slung the Range rover onto the driveway, with indecent haste he was out and opening the front door, his eyes feasting over Jeanette as she stood from her perch and sashayed towards him a smile on her freshly painted lips. "Someone's in a hurry" she teased "I'll just get my coat. Roger realised his wife had come in behind him and turned to her "Darling I am going to give the babysitter a lift home, why don't you make yourself comfortable, I'll be back within the hour and we can make a night of it" Ann pushed past him mumbling something about a headache and an early start, but Roger wasn't listening, clearing the doorway, he couldn't take his eyes of the tight young arse walking out to the car in front of him, His nuts tightened involuntarily. Christ he thought this is not going to take long, Selecting reverse he backed carefully off the drive and headed for a deserted house on the edge of the city he had seen earlier. Jeanette had hitched her skirt high up her thigh showing a glimpse of creamy thigh and the tops of her suspenders, the rustle as she ran her hands down her legs was torture to Roger who was struggling to concentrate on the road ahead. Rogers concentration took another hit when Jeannette's hand slid into his lap and gently scratched his balls "For three hundred, you can put it anywhere" she breathed into his ear twisting towards him on the cream leather seat showing more thigh and just a glimpse of her g string. Roger nodded his consent, the power of speech leaving him. His mouth was dry and he tried to gather the saliva needed to swallow with little success.

Ten minutes later he pulled into a quiet dark lane at the rear of an abandoned house, Jeanette had been alternating between stroking his cock and rubbing herself through her clothing and he felt he was going to explode he switched off the headlights swivelled in his seat and reached for Jeanette, coquettishly she moved away from him and said "Aren't you forgetting something" Roger grabbed at his clothing desperately looking for his wallet "It's £400 said Jeanette Roger pulling out his wallet replied "I thought it was £300" In answer Jeanette undid the button holding her skirt together and opened out the fabric, Rogers eyes bulged out of his head as he took in the gap between her thighs framed by the black stockings. Roger grabbed the handful of notes in his wallet and passed the lot to Jeanette who smiled at him as she leant forward putting the notes into the handbag on the floor in front of her. Straightening up and opening the door to the car she gave Roger a little wink "come on then stud, I've been here before the door is open and there is a mattress we will be much more comfortable in there" Roger unbuckled his safety belt and followed Jeanette into the property.

As she walked ahead of him into the property Jeanette began shedding clothing she knew she looked amazing in the half-light caused by street lighting diffusing through the gaps in the boarded up windows, after her orgasm earlier she was hoping Roger would be able to get her off at least once more, looking back at him over her shoulder as he hopped about discarding his own clothing Jeanette wasn't too sure he was going to last long enough to get his boxers off.

Turning towards him discarding her bra as she did so Jeanette enjoyed the feeling of power she held over Roger who was clearly desperate to fuck her She thought back to the first time she had fucked for money and her initial belief that it was a situation that gave all the power to the purchaser, looking down at Rogers throbbing erection she thought to herself that there was no contest over who held the balance of power in this situation, The creek of a floorboard elsewhere in the building startled her momentarily but she ignored it turning to Roger and saying "come on then are you going to fuck me or what" The sight of her tight high breasts with darkening nipples swollen in the cool air was all the encouragement Roger needed and discarding his underwear in a pile around his feet he reached for her feeling his stiff cock slide against the warm smoothness of her belly, Jeanette climbed up him wrapping her legs and arms around him, she moved her body in his arms so that his cock rubbed against the smooth satin of her g string "your already wet" remarked Roger "It's all for you baby" she replied ducking her head and biting his nipple with her sharp little teeth, Rogers breath hissed in his throat "come on take me in to that room there" Jeanette said indicating a closed door ahead "there's a mattress" holding her close to him Roger followed Jeanette's instructions entering the room and spotting the mattress in the corner loosened his grip on Jeanette's thighs and let her slide to the grubby mattress. Jeanette pulled him down with her and he went to his knees between her thighs, Placing her ankles on his shoulders she reached down and took hold of his cock surprised by the heat of it as she slid her g string to one side and slowly slid the head of hi cock the length of her wet slit, Roger let out a desperate growl and bucking his hips buried himself to the hilt into her tight pussy. Jeanette's eyes flew wide as he impaled her filling her with his bigger than she expected cock

Roger had been waiting a long time to bury his cock in her snatch and wasn't prepared to wait any longer he bucked his hips sliding almost fully out of Jeanette's warm pussy before sliding his full length back into her, Jeanette tightened herself around him as she did moving her legs behind his back scissoring him and locking him into her, in a few seconds she had gone from being totally in control of the situation to being trapped under Roger who was looking down on her furiously as he used her. Jeanette found that she liked it.

Roger moved his hand trying to target Jeanette's clit with her thumb, the change in her breathing let him know he was on target and he began to rub, Jeanette let a low moan escape her lips tilting her head back and moved her hands over her body squeezing her erect nipples between her fingers "Harder" she moaned as the smell of her cum made his nostrils flare as her slick juices coated his cock running down onto his balls. He looked over his shoulder at the small red light and winked at the camera.

Foxy's Story

Foxy couldn't believe his luck, ignoring the risk of splinters he had his eye glued to the cracked floorboard directly above the mattress in the room below, The girl from the library was naked below him squeezing her own tits and getting fucked by some bloke, Quickly he adjusted his clothing exposing himself. Reaching into the deep pocket of his coat he pulled out the underwear he had stolen earlier and put it to his nose inhaling the smell of dried cum and cunt. He began slowly to slide his hand along the length of his cock in time with the thrusts of the man below, he watched as he slid full length out of the girl and flipped her over pressing her face down into the mattress and used a hand to use some of her own juices to lube her little puckered arse hole. Yes thought Foxy that's exactly what I would do he squeezed his cock a bit harder, the girl gasped as the man's cock slid into her arse. Foxy felt the building pressure in his balls signalling he was going to cum and slowed his strokes, just like the man below who was now sliding in and out of that tight little arse and using his hand to rub the girls clit "Do you fucking love it" he heard the man say his voice rough with lust "tell me you fucking love it" the girl screamed orgasmic, bucking on the mattress and staring up at him with unseeing eyes.

The man was sweating and Foxy kept pulling his cock faster and faster enjoying the show, he sniffed deeply on the knickers in his left hand imagining he had his face buried in the wet snatch of the girl spread below him, The man had now pulled out of her arse and was busy coaxing the girl to mount him as he lay back on the mattress, Foxy was fighting a losing battle to delay his own pleasure stuffing the knickers deep into his mouth to muffle his own screams as he surfed the waves of pleasure and came.

Roger & Jeanette's story

Jeanette couldn't believe that Roger had made her cum twice and was still rock hard, she had seriously seriously got this one wrong but as he pulled her on top of him and she impaled herself on his throbbing cock she knew this was her chance to take control, Slowing her movements down she rubbed herself up and down his length and leant forward over him letting her swollen nipple rub his chest and her long hair cascade over his face, taking his hands she pinned him to the mattress and leaned back changing the angle so that the head of his cock rubbed hard against her pelvic bone, speeding up and leaning back further and further increasing the friction between their bodies she felt Roger begin to tense below her "Fucking cum for me, I want to feel you explode inside me" She gasped her own breathing ragged "Dirty fucking slag" Roger replied "Your loving this" he bucked his hips burying himself to the hit inside her letting out a roar as he came, throwing his head back as he did so he felt something warm splatter against his face falling from the roof above too far gone to care as Jeanette tightened up around him milking him of every last drop. The feel of his hot seed filling her made another orgasm rush up on her and she screamed.

Collapsing back onto the mattress Jeanette's panting slowed as her breathing came under control "Wow" she said out loud to nobody in particular thinking to herself that maybe she should be giving Roger a refund. She had seriously misjudged him. Roger lifted himself onto an elbow next to him in order to look down on her body "Enjoy yourself?" he smirked absent minded licking at a dribble of fluid that had made its way off his cheek , "what the fuck" he mumbled "how the fuck did I get cum on my own face" Jeanette giggled then screamed as her eyes suddenly focussed on the hole in the roof above her, she heard a rustle of clothing a bump and the sound of scampering feet followed by a slam and the noise of an engine starting out on the street. As she came to terms with what she had just seen she watched another globule of fluid detach itself from the ceiling and fall onto Rogers upturned face.

Brenda's story

Today was Thursday and it was an excited Brenda who locked the door to the Plaice. Today was delivery day. Turning the fryers off Brenda went through to the rear of the shop listening intently for the sound of the diesel van that would signify that Eric the potato man had arrived. Brenda didn't really care that the rumour was the Eric had women all over Hull and if the rumours were to be believed even had a monthly liaison with a landlady in Grimsby. All Brenda knew was that with today's picky youth it was getting harder and harder to find a willing accomplice to her mid-week shenanigans.

It never used to be like this, Brenda mused as she mushed the peas. She recalled a time when she first started working at The Plaice when she had her pick of fellas; all it took was an extra scoop of chips to let a young lothario know she was keen, and she could expect a proposition later in the evening. Such was Brenda's appetite that she got through a lot of chips. Unfortunately It wasn't just her sexual appetite that Brenda was able to suppress with Chips, constant munching had destroyed the figure she was sure she used to have leaving her overweight with a saggy arse. Spending so long in an atmosphere that was 30% pure dripping had also left their mark, Brenda's pudgy fingers again lifted up her blouse to scratch at the latest outbreak along the edge of her muffin top.

An hour later and with the peas mushed, and the last of the sweepings put in a pile for use later that evening Brenda was getting impatient "Wheear is t' clart noggin if 'e's not eear soon ah shall start wiyaa'im" She muttered kicking out at a sack of peelings. Suddenly feeling naughty Brenda kicked off her flats and unbuttoning her blouse peeling it from her sweaty back before flinging it across the small kitchen, Breathing in she got enough slack in the waist of her trousers to slip the button allowing her massive bottom to spring free. It took considerable effort for her then to drag them to her ankles over her ample thighs. Finally free Brenda jumped up on a work surface facing the rear door that would be Eric's route to the kitchen.⏎

Ann's story

Ann had been busy this morning, working on her latest project and she was satisfied with the results, she didn't particularly like her husband anymore but she had to admit he still had presence and stamina. And his idea to make use of her media skills to film porno's had turned into a real eye opener for Ann.

About two years ago Ann had arrived home early from a trip away filming, surprised to find her husband's car on the drive in the middle of the day she had let herself into the house and found Roger with his face buried between the thighs of another woman, Ann Had watched mesmerised as her husband had made the woman cum several times with his tongue before flipping her over and fucking her for several minutes; before with her camera running she had walked in on them. Her initial intention had been just to scare Roger but seeing him react positively to the camera had given her an idea. Ann had been involved in several one night stands on her travels to this point but had always been uncomfortable with the sneaking around. Suggesting to Roger that he could fuck who he liked, just as long as she could watch and film it Ann felt evened things up a bit. From there it was only a matter of time till they started to sell the videos on the internet. The capitalist in Roger realised that by making the videos free to anyone meant that they could sell advertising space alongside to the highest bidder.

Uploading the latest video to the site she expected the royalties to surpass all the others. The baby sitter was cute she thought to herself. I wonder if she has ever had a woman.

Eric's story

Eric lit his roll up swung the first sack of spuds off the tailgate of his wagon and balancing easily against the load walked through the rear door of 'The plaice' and stopped. Spread across the counter in front of him in all her womanly glory was Brenda "Bloody 'ell relic theur av eur cunt li' eur badly wrapped kebab" He grinned hungrily at her dropping his load to the floor, his cock slowly stiffening in his overalls "Wha' theur waitin for cum 'eear 'n gi' uz um o' 'a' sausage" breathed Brenda hoarsely spreading her legs, Eric didn't need further invitation and stepped towards her "Fookin' 'ell" He said unzipping and stepping out of his overalls "that's eur greetin lass ah'm goan quid theur gormless" He said lifting his paunch and dragging his Y fronts down to his knees His cock springing straight to attention pulling the foreskin to reveal the cratered head he said "Ah'm goan warm dis up i' thy cunt then thy goan suk it dry" Brenda smiled encouragingly "Ok then gurt lad cum 'n gerr uz kitty 'asn't bin fed today" Eric lifted his hands to Brenda's massive dugs and proceeded with his standard foreplay of massaging them for a few moments before losing interest lifting his belly and grabbing his now solid cock aimed it at Brenda's flaps and slid it home, She was loose but wet and willing every holes a cunt thought Eric and pumped away, while sucking his roll up.

"Gi' wee eur kiss theur sexy beast" gasped Brenda lost in her own romantic fantasy, Eric pumping away grimaced "Thy breyth smells o' farts ah'm just 'a fert fookin" dispelling any thought of romance, Brenda didn't care she was lost in her own fantasy, She didn't hear Eric's coarseness, the squeeks of her saggy arse against the metal counter surface and the sucking wet slaps of their fucking. After a couple of minute's Eric pulled out "Gue on then gerr thy gob aroun' 'a' ah'm not goan last much longa" Brenda's arse squeaked as she slipped off the counter onto the floor her face coming level with

Eric's swinging cock, oblivious to the smell she took him into her mouth and sucked hard swallowing him to the hilt before she let her tongue swirl around the tip, taking it right to the back of her throat she stroked his saggy ball sack with her other hand "Agh thy goan mek uz cum" wheezed Eric his balls tightening Brenda moved her hand to his shaft and began to wank him expertly "Spaff on uz bastard tits" She said looking up at him. It was too much for Eric so he obliged her request and dropped his load all over her tits with a shudder.

Hoisting his trousers and refastening his belt Eric took one look at Brenda rubbing his cum into her wrinkly cleavage "Reet then love sem tahhm next week" and relighting his roll up from a gas burner he strolled back out of the kitchen got into his wagon and was gone.

Foxy's Story

The following Wednesday at two o'clock Foxy walked into Albion street library, His favourite Blonde Librarian was on duty as usual and this time as he looked her up and down he grinned to himself, safe in the knowledge that he knew exactly what was under her jeans and sweater. Paying for his internet with a spunk encrusted fiver he shuffled over to his usual machine and logged on.

www.freepornslags.com/dirtybitches

Selecting recent video's his eyes widened when he saw what was displayed, he then began to laugh

Jeanette's story

Having just settled down to view her internet banking Jeanette was started by the hacking and wheezing noise coming from the homeless man she had just taken the suspiciously crust fiver off. Concerned that a death in the library might scupper her evenings plans she decided to go and check he was ok. As she approached she saw that his shoulders were shaking and suddenly realised that he was laughing. Continuing up behind him she immediately noticed the cock in his hand, but before she had time to take this in she noticed what he was watching on the scream. Jeanette began to scream.

17152717R00031

Printed in Poland
by Amazon Fulfillment
Poland Sp. z o.o., Wrocław